When in the Course of Human Events

Independence from Political Parties

John Smallwood

authorHOUSE®

AuthorHouse™
1663 Liberty Drive
Bloomington, IN 47403
www.authorhouse.com
Phone: 1-800-839-8640

First published by AuthorHouse 5/20/2009

ISBN: 978-1-4389-8046-1 (sc)
ISBN: 978-1-4389-8047-8 (e)

Printed in the United States of America
Bloomington, Indiana

This book is printed on acid-free paper.

Political parties by their actions have created "a house divided against itself"

"A government of the people by the people and for the people shall not perish from this earth"

Lincoln

Preface

This manuscript is an attempt to inspire the American citizenry to renew the belief in the American dream (their dream not some organized political party), and the American democratic process (now manipulated by political parties). It is not intended to be a civics or history lesson. It is intended to pattern a new "Declaration of Independence" based on the original declaration. The American citizenry and political processes have changed. It is dedicated to all Americans, past and present, for participating in this political and social experiment of a "government of the people, by the people, and for the people", and the hope it shall not perish from this

This book has only one purpose:

Encourage every eligible American citizen to be a participant in this on-going experiment of self-government, and propose the changes necessary to allow all American citizens to equally participate in their relationship with their government.

But understand

It can still fail!!!

Lincoln believed:
America is the world's last great hope for freedom on this earth

On July 4, 2009, the American public will join together to, as Martin Luther (start of the Protestant movement) did many years ago:

> Join with other citizens in mass, and take this "Declaration, to every state capital and the capital of the United States and nail this document to the buildings. A legal act of "protest for change".

> We must take back our government from the "political bands", and inform them of our grievances as Thomas Jefferson instructed.

In

1776

Each state will require a leader, an effective organization, and functioning plans to make this happen. Their must be hundreds of thousands Americans involved.

This will be an organized protest of the status of a government controlled by political parties not by the citizens entrusted to represent!

I may be reached by e-mail at governmentchains@yahoo.com for any assistance or questions.

http//www.govchains-politicalparties.blogspot.com

Forward

We were taught in our schools the start of the "independence" movement in the United States was the result of "taxation without representation". This certainly does not do justice to the intellectual capacities of our founding fathers. I believe, actually taught, it was once said by John F. Kennedy during a cabinet meeting in the White House dining room, that, "there has not been so much intellect in this room since Thomas Jefferson ate here alone."

The concepts and ideas, of government are as old as the beginning of man on this earth. And yes, the concept of democracy is just as old. The Greek philosophers expounded on the virtues, or inadequacies, of democratic governments. Plato theorized in the "Republic" democracy assumed citizens were not aware of what society needed to survive. In the "Republic" there were ideal citizens (soldiers and common people) and elite guardians (philosophers) of the society trained for the task of governing. Individual freedoms and rights are of little consequence because the guardians "know what is best". Was this the beginning of political parties, because they certainly legislate as if "they know best"!!

America is a "representative democracy" (participation by the legal citizens through free elections choosing representatives to represent them regarding their governance). It should be noted, America is not the first democratic government. There have been others that have failed. Democracies fail for many reasons, but I would postulate, "Democracies fail when the legal citizens of that democracy are restricted from exercising their rights or the citizens of that democracy, because of citizenry apathy, no longer participate and allow the ruling class (political parties) control over their freedoms."

Let no law or political process be enacted that restricts the right to vote

Let no government create apathy among the citizens

A problem cannot be properly addressed with limited knowledge of the processes. Ignore these processes and a government takes another form.

Chapter 1

The Declaration of Independence will take most Americans less than 15 minutes to read. The following are some highlights:

1). "When in the course of human events, it becomes necessary for one people to dissolve the "political bands" which have connected them with another...seeking separate and equal station to which the laws of nature and nature's god entitled them"

Notice: the reference to political bands... not governments... This simply recognizes that governments are constitued by political bands... and these political bands may not have.... A decent respect to the opinions of mankind"... or the citizens that are governed.

2). "We hold these truths to be self-evident, that all men are created equal, that they are endowed by their creator with certain unalienable (not to be taken away) rights, that among these are life, liberty, and the pursuit of happiness". But: the reality of human existence is all men are not created under equal circumstances. And it is the circumstances to exercise these rights that governments are instituted to secure (not limit except as agreed by those governed). "That to secure these rights, governments are instituted among men, deriving their "just" powers from the consent of the governed, …. That whenever any form of government, or political process becomes destructive of these ends, it is the "right" of the people to alter or to abolish it".

Notice: the preferred method of change is through the electoral process, or voting, but as has been seen throughout history (and certainly the American experience) insurrection may be required. Governments should establish laws allowing a man/woman born of any circumstance to exercise their unalienable rights of life, liberty, and the pursuit of happiness equally!!!

3). …"accordingly all experience hath shown, that mankind are more disposed to suffer, while evils are sufferable, than to right themselves by abolishing the forms to which they are accustomed. But, when a long train of ineffective government, it is their duty to throw off such government".

Notice: In the United States each election is the opportunity to continue the freedom revolution began on July, 4, 1776, but the people must be heard, and voting is the method to express discontent, and when necessary make changes!!! This is why the freedom to vote in "free" elections is paramount to the success of any democracy.

4). In the beginning of this exercise, I eluded to the "taxation without representation" reason for the separation and war with England. But the Declaration of Independence actually lists 27 reasons. Yes, 27 reasons. "for imposing taxes on us without our consent", is actually number 17. The first three reasons deal specifically with the nature of laws passed, denied, or even ignored.

Notice: in the United States, tax laws are passed by the legislative branches of our government with the members of that legislative branch elected in "free" elections.

The history of the United States pursuit of individual freedom for the citizens of the United States has recorded three major events: the Revolutionary War for Independence, the Civil War fought over the rights of freedoms for all United States citizens, and the Civil Rights Movement of the 1960's for equality of all races. It is notable major changes in the United States historically are brought about through violence of the citizens against their government, seeking equal rights for all citizens and ensuring the right of all those citizens the right to vote in "free" elections.

Chapter 2

Taking a view of revising the "Declaration of Independence", a review of what could be logically concluded regarding the intent of the document.

1.) "When in the course of human events" could today be worded …

   Revise: When in the course of human understanding of events. Simply because the "political bands" may, in fact, disparage those events to misdirect, or blur the events…negating the "people's" ability to grasp the event(s).

2.) "It becomes necessary for one people to dissolve the "political bands" which have connected them with another"
   Clearly Jefferson intentionally did not use the word "governments", but chose to use "political bands". He later refers to "governments" as institutions, but here he states a clear understanding of the role of "political parties".

Revise: this statement should not be revised. It defines the relationship between "government" and those who wish to control the "government" the "political parties".

3.) "And to assume among the powers of the earth, the separate and equal station to which the laws of nature and of nature's god entitle them, a decent respect to the opinions of mankind requires that they should declare the causes which impel them to the "separation".

Revise: "And to assume among the powers of the earth, the separate and equal station entitled to the consent of the governed by the laws of nature and nature's creator, a respect and reasonable understanding of the opinions of society requires that they should declare the abuses of both "political" and "governmental" powers which impel them to separation. Separation may be effected either by vote of the governed or armed resurrection as required by the response of the "political bands".

4.) " We hold these truths to be self-evident"

Revise: "We hold these truths to be inherently self-evident.

5.) "That all men are created equal",

Revise: that all human beings are created equal in their relationship with "government"

6.) "That they are endowed by their creator with certain unalienable rights, that among these are life, liberty and the pursuit of happiness",

Revise: "That they are endowed at their creation with certain unalienable rights, privileges and responsibilities, that among these are life, liberty and the pursuit of happiness.

7.) "That to secure these rights, governments are instituted among men, deriving their just powers from the consent of the governed",

Revise: that to secure these rights and privileges governments are instituted among men/women, deriving their just powers from the acknowledged consent of the governed.

8.) "That whenever any form of government becomes destructive of these ends it is the right of the people to alter or to abolish it",

Revise: "That whenever any form of government, or "political bands", become destructive of these ends it is the "right and responsibility" of the citizens to alter or abolish them."

9.) "And to institute new government, laying its foundation on such principles and organizing its powers in such form, as to them shall seem most likely to effect their safety and happiness",

Revise: "And to institute new, or alter the existing government/political bands, laying its foundation on such principles and organizing its powers, and access to those powers in such form, as to them shall seem most likely to effect their safety and happiness."

10.) "Prudence, indeed, will dictate that governments long established should not be changed for light and transient causes; and accordingly all experience hath shewn, that mankind are more disposed to suffer, while the evils are sufferable, than to right themselves by abolishing the forms to which they are accustomed. But when a long train of abuses and usurpations, pursuing invariably the same object evinces a design to reduce them under absolute despotism, it is their right, it is their duty to throw off such government, and to provide new guards for their future security"

Revise: "Prudence, indeed, will dictate that governments long established should not be changed for light and transient causes; history has recorded that human beings are more disposed to suffer, while evils are sufferable making the abolishment, or alteration of those governments, or political bands, extremely more difficult and more violent. But when a long train of abuses and usurpations, pursuing invariably the same object evinces a design to reduce them under despotism, it is their unalienable right and it is their responsibility (duty) to throw off such government, or disband the political bands, and to provide new guards for their future security."

Chapter 3

Therefore

The following would be the revised "Declaration of Independence" with the goal of a call to action by the constitutionally legal citizens of the United States of America to "list the charges against the "political bands" which demonstrate they have violated the "rights" of the American citizens and are therefore given until the election of 2010 to resolve the charges or be denied the opportunity to continue their control over the "governance" of these United States of america.

This is not a call to change the concept of a "representative democracy", but a change in the process of how those in power, the "political bands", (now to be referred to as "political parties", or "they") administer their duties and responsibilities which can simply be the words of the preamble of the united states constitution: (1) in order to form a more perfect union, (2) establish justice, (3) insure domestic tranquility, (4) provide for the common defence, (5) promote the general welfare, and (6) secure the blessings of liberty to ourselves and our posterity.

As Jean-Jacques Rousseau wrote, "Man was born free, and he is everywhere in chains. Those who think themselves the masters of others are indeed greater slaves than they". The political parties have developed party processes that require "free thinkers" to acquiesce to the party processes or become a non-participant in governance.

Declaration of Independence

Issued on July 4, 2009

When in the course of human events as understood by legally recognized citizens of any nation (recognized by the community of nations) it becomes necessary for one people to dissolve the "political parities" control which have connected them with their government, and to assume among the powers of the earth, separated and equal station entitled to the consent of the governed by the laws of nature and nature's creator, respect and reasonable understanding of the opinions of society requires that they should declare the abuses of political and governmental powers which impel them to separation. Separation may be effected either by a vote of the governed or by armed insurrection as required by the response of the "political parties", of the government.

We hold these truths to be inherently self-evident, that all human beings are created equal in their participation and relationship with their "government", that they are endowed at their creation with certain unalienable rights, privileges and responsibilities, that among these are life, liberty and the pursuit of happiness, that to secure the free exercise of these rights, privileges and responsibilities, governments are instituted among men/women, deriving their just powers from the acknowledged consent of the governed. Whenever any form of government, or those "political parties", becomes destructive of these ends, it is the "right and responsibility" of the citizens to alter or abolish them. And to institute new, or alter the existing government/political parties laying their foundation on such principles and organizing its powers and access to those powers in such form, as to them shall seem most likely to affect their "safety and happiness". Prudence, indeed, will dictate that governments/political parties long established should not be changed for light and transient causes; history has recorded that human beings are more disposed to suffer, while evils are sufferable, making the abolishment, or alteration of those governments/political parties more difficult and more violent. But when a long train of abuses and usurpations, pursuing invariably the same object evinces a design to reduce them under despotism, it is the right and it is their responsibility (duty) to current and future human beings to throw off such government, or disband the "political parties", and to provide new guards for their future security.

Such has been the extreme patient suffrage of the citizens of the United States of America and all human existence under a government manipulated by "political parties" that puts the citizens in chains; and such is now the necessity which constrains them to alter the control of the "political parties" in order for a return to the established government processes detailed in the "Constitution of the United States of America". The history of the "political parties" of the United States is a history of repeated injuries and usurpations, all having the direct object of reducing the involvement of the citizens of the United States of America, all having in direct object the establishment of a totalitarian state. (By definition, totalitarianism is a concept used to describe political systems whereby a state regulates nearly every aspect of public and private life, and it can be the result of a "free" voting process. A totalitarian politicizes (by secularizing) everything spiritual and human. Totalitarian regimes or "political parties" maintain themselves in political power by means of an official all-embracing ideology and propaganda (maybe state controlled); with one or two major parties that controls the state, personality cults, control over the economy, regulation and restriction of free discussion and criticism.

To substantiate this, let facts be submitted to a candid world:

1.) The political parties (now referred to "they") control through manipulation the voting process which is a basic freedom granted to the citizens of a democracy by:

A. The voter registration of the legal citizens of the United States is now left to organizations with political interest, not the legal framework of the constitution. The right to vote, carries a responsibility to vote, must be protected by the laws of the United States with clear guidelines and no intervention by organizations with political interests. It is the right to vote!!

B. To protect the right to vote, laws must be enacted and enforcement guaranteed that establish punishment for any violation of that right. The right to vote is a basic principle of our system of governance and is not to be manipulated.

C. A candidate shall only seek one elective office in any election process.

D. If a candidate chooses to seek an office other than the one currently elected, they must resign the current elected office.

E. Elections shall be held on two consecutive weekend days allowing for an increased opportunity for maximum participation of the citizens right to vote

F. Political affiliation of a candidate shall not be indicated in any manner on any ballot

G. All current technology shall be used to assure all living legal citizens, not residents but legal citizens, the right to vote when an election is held on the federal, state and local levels.

H. They shall pass a law respecting the use of the "secret" ballot for all elective processes in the United States. A principle necessary for the democratic process to survive.

I. They will pass laws specifying punishment for voting violations protecting the right of one man/woman one vote

J. They will establish an election process, by law that will limit primary campaigning to three months, and elective campaigning to three months.

K. They will control the above by allowing no spending other than the equally allocated government funds.

L. They will pass a law allowing all legal voters to participate in all primary campaigns.

M. They will pass legislation that will, without limiting "free speech" deny access to the elective and legislative processes by denying contributions to political parties. Access to the electorate directly cannot be denied.

N. They will not have by-laws that deny the number of candidates to campaign for an office during the primary campaigns, and will support all candidates equally through the campaign process. Where only one candidate is announced, no monies will be allocated during the primary campaigns

O. They will establish a structure of campaign contributions whereby monies will be donated to the federal, state and local government to be equally distributed during the election cycle.

P. They will allow the names of the two candidates, from each political party, gaining the highest number of votes to run in the general elections.

2.) They have refused their assent to the laws, the most necessary for the public good, such as the right to bear arms, laws governing citizenship, and the definition of citizenship

3.) they have usurped the rights of the member states to govern effectively

4.) they have borrowed money from the citizens and used these monies for other purposes than stated

5.) they have, by lack of enforcement, effectively suspended laws properly instituted.

6.) they hold secret meetings that impact the legislation imposed on the citizens

7.) they have altered "equal access" to the political processes effectively altering "equal access" to the government

8.) They have obstructed the administration of justice by politizing the appointment of justices

9.) they have not enforced the laws of immigration or laws of naturalization.

10.) they have erected a multitude of new offices growing the breadth of government control, ignoring the instruction of the preamble to the constitution

11.) they have spent the money of the citizens creating a deficit with no viable plan to erase that deficit

12.) they have imposed taxes (some in the form of fees) on the citizens without consent and many times without transparency

13.) they have allowed access to our judicial process to individuals and organizations not constitutionally having such access

14.) they have denied the right of the citizens to vote on powerful legislative positions making those positions answerable to the "political parties", not the citizens

15.) they have not taken advantage of technology that would allow greater participation in the processes of governance

16.) they "provide" the "general welfare" rather than "promote" it. Robert Nozick is credited with writing (paraphrased), "the welfare state is legally institutionalized theft, to it would be true progressive taxation is a form of forced labor"

17.) they have designed a tax system and code to support that system that dispels the foundation of our system of governing principles. All citizens should enjoy the blessing of liberty. The tax law regarding the levy and collection of income taxes should be uniform for all citizens. Simplicity would dictate (a) a flat tax of 10% levied on all income earners and (b) a user tax designed to correct (not compensate) for any inherent inequities due to income stratification. These taxes will be collected and paid at the point of transaction negating the need for the filing of individual income taxes.

18.) they have violated the intent of section 8 of the constitution by non-uniformity of the excise taxes and bracketed income tax levy

19.) they have created an 80,000 page tax code allowing for the maipulation of the tax system creating an "inequality".

20.) they have refused to investigate and duly punish their members who have been elected

21.) they have refused to exercise the constitutional right of the Vice-President to be the president of the senate.

22.) they have taken actions both politically and financially that do not secure the "posterity" (preamble of the constitution) of the United States of America

24.) they have established congressional districts that favor the "political parties" not the free flow of ideas about governance (gerrymandering)

25.) they have misconstrued the actual language of the constitution taking linguistic liberty (not constitutionally a guaranteed right) with words and statements.

26.) they have passed laws that, are, in fact, unconstitutional without attempting to amend the constitution.

27.) they have passed laws that intrude on the private lives of citizens

28.) they have fundamentally altered the forms of the government

29.) they have passed laws and resolutions which cause discrimination of individuals and classes of individuals. Quote from John Rawls, "no one knows their place in society....nor does anyone know their fortune in the distribution of natural assets and abilities", but under no circumstance do political parties define.

30.) they have taken a government designed on the basic principle of freedom and politicized each action simply meaning they have made us believe for one to "gain a right" another must "sacrifice a right"

31.) they shall propose, or amend, the XII amendment no longer requiring "electors" which has inherent "equality" issues.

32.) they shall return to the principle the Vice-President" is an elective office, not a partnership with the president.

33.) they shall change the equation for the apportionment of members of the house of representatives. This equation should be based on a relationship of square miles and population. The current system causes "inequalities" in the "federalist" system…."A more perfect union".

34.) they shall correct the succession to the presidency, stipulating anyone in the succession to the presidency must be selected by a vote of the majority of Americans; therefore, if the speaker of the house of representatives is in the succession line, they must be on a national ballot… not a political party designate

Therefore: let it be known to all citizens of the United States and those serving a political party in government, the elected members will be allowed to address, or alter, their actions according to the above abuses by the election cycle of 2010. If this is not done all connections between the citizens of the United States and political parties will be dissolved.

Chapter 4

The Constitution
Of the
United States
Of
America

The Constitution of the United States is one of
the most clearly written documents in history.
It is a tribute to the intellect of the authors that
is such a short concise document they were
able to create a system of government that has
lasted over 200 years, and continues to survive.
It has only been amended 27 times. Note: the
"political parties" and the legal profession have
taken poetic linguistic license with the words;
therefore the document has been changed
in meaning because of the interpretation of
"words"

The beginning:

"We the people of the United States, in order
to form a more perfect union establish justice,
insure domestic tranquility, provide for the

common defence, promote the general welfare, and secure the blessings of liberty to ourselves and our posterity, do ordain and establish this Constitution for the United States."

The more perfect union is what we know as the "federalist system", where power is shared between local, state and a federal government. Whereby some rights are strictly reserved for the member States, and some are shared with the Federal government. Section 8 of article 1 of the constitution detail the specific powers granted to the Federal government, the other rights are reserved strictly to the States unless elected representatives of those states by a majority vote agree to share or surrender those rights. History would detail the States have surrendered more power to the federal government due to the "inequality" of the apportionment of votes in the legislative branch of the federal government.

Establishing justice has created an enormous legal profession. Justice can be defined as: (a) social justice, (b) poetic justice, (c) criminal justice, (d) environmental justice, (e) legal justice, (f) distributive justice, (g) economic justice, (h) compensation justice...just to name a few. The constitutional intent was either fairness, or establishes a system of law in which each citizen receives their due process from the system, including all rights both natural and legal (West's Encyclopedia of American Law) as defined by the established laws approved either by the federal/state governments or a direct vote by the citizens.

Insuring domestic tranquility specifically would be enumerated in Article 1 Section 8: "to provide for the calling forth the militia to execute the laws of the union, suppress insurrection and repel invasions."

"provide for the common defence" with details again in Article 1 with several entries such as the power to borrow money, to coin money, to declare war, raise armies, etc.

"promote the general welfare", notice specifically above the use of provide, and here the use of promote. To promote means to "make available", to provide means "to get possession of by doubtful means or ingenuity".

"and to secure the blessings of liberty to ourselves and our posterity"… not prosperity!

The constitution establishes a government with "checks and balances". Simply put, the design of the government invests specific powers of government with three branches of government, an executive, legislative and judicial. Each branch has a check on the other to ensure one does not have absolute power.

Article 1:

Provides the framework for the legislative branch of our government to make all the laws on a federal level. It sets the standards, processes, election times etc. Yes, all laws, this is not a power granted to the President or the Supreme Court. Laws such as, lay and collect taxes, duties, imposts and excises, to borrow money on the credit of the united states, to regulate commerce, to establish a uniform rule of naturalization, to coin money, to constitute tribunals inferior to the supreme court, all bills raising revenue shall originate in the congress. Note: the duties of the Vice-President are only enumerated in Article 1 other than succession of the President in case of death or incapacitation. The Vice-President is the President of the Senate, but shall have no vote, unless they be equally divided...the President Pro-Tempore clearly has no duties except in the absence of the Vice-President. The political parties have changed this constitutional safe guard.

Article 2:

Provides the framework for the executive branch

of the government. The President must be a natural born citizen of the United States (so the succession of the presidency cannot have a person who is not a naturalized citizen). The three major powers of the president enumerated in the constitution are: (a) commander-in-chief (article 2 section 1) and (b) he shall take care that the laws be faithfully executed (article 2 section 3), and nomination of supreme court justices (article 2 section 2). Not a power but enumerated responsibility…"he shall from time to time give to Congress information of the State of the Union, and recommend to their consideration such measures as he shall judge necessary and expedient…"

Article 3:

Does not specifically provide a framework for the judiciary branch, but does simply state, "the judicial power shall extend to all cases, in law and equity, arising under this Constitution". In other words, the Supreme Court (notable: the only court established in the constitution) interprets any law that may be in violation of the rights established by the Constitution. The term of service is not enumerated, only the statement…."Which shall not be diminished during their continuance in office". Access to the judgment of the Supreme Court is therefore only granted to citizens of the United States guaranteed by the constitution. The Congress has enhanced the power of the judiciary by expanding the number of courts. The legal profession has enhanced the judicial power with the application of "judicial precedence".

Article 4:

Provides a definition of the meaning of a federalist system explaining the rights of the member States and the citizens of those States. Note: this article was amended by the 13th amendment to the constitution.

Article 5:

This article deals specifically with the amendment process of the constitution. Note: "and that no state, without its consent, shall be deprived of its equal suffrage in the Senate". Is this an acknowledgement of the inequality of suffrage in the House of Representatives? This acknowledgement resulted in the passing of the 17th amendment, but historically this amendment has constitutionality issues, specifically the election process of members of the senate.

Article 6:

This is where you will find the statement:

this constitution and the laws of the United States shall be "the supreme law of the land"(Supremacy Clause). It further states all duly elected officials, either federal or state, are bound by oath or affirmation, to support this Constitution; but no religious test shall ever be required as a qualification to any office or public trust under the United States. Is this stipulating a "limitmus test" is a "religious test"?

Linguistic license???

Article 7

Details the ratification of the Constitution.

Chapter 5

The amendments:

Why a defined amendment process?

"a desire, in order to prevent misconstruction or abuse of powers, that further declaratory and restrictive clauses should be added, note: and as extending the ground of public confidence in the government, will best ensure the beneficent ends of its institution".

An amendment is called an "article" until they were legally approved as an amendment.

First article, not ratified, dealt with the number of representatives in the House of Representatives. This article stipulated no less than 100 (1 for every 30,000 legal citizens), and after reaching 200 (no less than one for every 50,000). It probably failed due to the inequality of the apportionment of number of house members. This is still an issue today stated as: the inequality of representation of member states in the legislative branch, or law making branch of the federalist system.

The second article, not ratified, was concerned with compensation for the legislative members. Although it failed during the ratification of the constitution, it was later passed as the 27th amendment.

First amendment:

No law respecting an establishment of religion, or prohibiting the free exercise thereof (this is pretty clear, no law!! A law restricts or defines a judicial decision, or interpretation assumes there is a law), freedom of speech (not freedom of expression), press and peaceful assembly. This amendment did not stipulate on public land such as public schools or government institutions. This amendment has been changed through judicial interpretation and later judicial precedence.

Second amendment:

A well regulated militia, being necessary to the security of a free state, the right of the people to keep and bear arms, shall not be infringed. The revolutionary war was one by citizens who owned guns and used them to repel the invasion of the English. These citizens owned and bore arms before the invasion. The government has no right to deny or make laws that infringe this right by defining types of "arms", number of "arms', etc. Actually the requirement of a "conceal and carry" license is a violation of this amendment, because the amendment stipulates to "bear" arms. Linguistic license has been taken by the "political parties" first to ignore the amendment process, and by passing laws that weaken this right to the citizens

Third amendment:

Right against the quartering of soldiers in any house. Certainly the result of the British forcing home owners in America to quarter soldiers. America was no longer an English colony, yet Americans were forced to house British soldiers during the revolutionary war.

Fourth amendment:

Would be called the "right to privacy" amendment, although it could be said the first 5 amendments address a person's privacy. Note: the constitution never uses the words "right to privacy". Simply meaning that probable cause is needed before the government may conduct a legal search of the private effects of a person including a search of the person. This is a contentious amendment because privacy is legally interpretative. The fact that a people make a "social contract" with a government to organize and secure society, is a surrendering of privacy. In order to participate in the basic "right to vote", the citizens must surrender anonymity. The payment of taxes is a surrender of privacy.... We actually inform the government of our income. In order to receive benefits from the government, we must "register". To drive a car, we must gain a driver's license. What privacy rights would we surrender to be "secure in our persons"?

Fifth Amendment:

Referred to as the "due process" amendment. Concerns with indictment by a grand jury for a capital crime, double jeopardy, not to be a witness against his/her self, and also, not to be denied of life, liberty or property without due process. Note: should the government be allowed to take a citizen's private property and sell for owed taxes? Is this "just" compensation, because the private property is taken for public use for payment of taxes. This amendment requires some clarity, but not just by judicial review.

Sixth amendment:

Also known as the "equal protection" amendment. Simply put this is the protection clause of the accused person. Highlighting speedy trial, impartial jury and right to mee accusers.

Seventh amendment:

This amendment is concerned with suits of common law exceeding $20. Such suits maintain the right of trial by jury. Note: "and no fact tried by a jury, shall be otherwise re-examined in any court of the United States, than according to the rules of the common law", such as the withholding of evidence. Why do we hear of so few attorneys being punished for the abuse of evidence information of common law cases?? Should not a judicial action be the search for "truth"?? The rights of the accused are protected that the truth is entered in evidence.

Eighth amendment:

Protects against excessive bail, fines, and cruel and unusual punishment. Note: this applies only to the citizens of the United States of America. Non-citizens or foreigners may not be allowed legal standing in a US court unless invited by the action. And when in such actions those persons will not be guaranteed the rights to (a) privacy, (b) due process and (c) equal protection

Ninth amendment:

Is probably more reflective of the first amendment, simply meaning the constitution shall not be used to deny or disparage rights retained by the people. Again, the rights retained by the legal citizens of the United States

Tenth amendment:

The powers not specifically delegated to the central government are reserved to the member states. Think of it simply as the states rights amendment. Clearly this amendment does not provide for powers on the United States government to be granted to any foreign governments, or foreign organizations.

Eleventh amendment:

"The judicial power of the United States shall not be construed to extend to any suit in law or equity, commenced or prosecuted against one of the United States by citizens of another state, or by citizens or subjects of any foreign state".

Twelfth amendment"

Established the "electoral college" for the election of the President and the Vice-President. Note: the amendment focuses on the President, but the language implies the Vice-President is getting votes for the office of the Vice-President...not as the "running mate" with the President.

Thirthteenth amendment:

This amendment legally, if not socially, abolished slavery. Historical significance: the original proposed article intended to be the 13th amendment (proposed in 1861 and endorsed by Lincoln while President-elect) denied the congress the authority to abolish or interfere, with any state regarding persons held to labor or service by the laws of said state!!!

Fourteenth amendment:

This amendment defines United States citizenship and stipulates no state may make laws that deny the privileges and immunities of citizens of the United States. Establishes the age of 21 for men (not women) for guaranteed voting rights. Explains how the population is counted to establish the number of electors for national elections. Note: Section 4 of this amendment states "the debt of the United States governement shall not be questioned". Wow!!! Slipped this in. Equally important: a violation of the oath of office to support the constitution shall not hold any office as a member of congress.... Is political pandering against the laws and constitution a violation of the oath of office?

Fifteenth amendment:

States the right to vote is not to be denied to citizens of the United States based on race or color. Note historical comment: when a new group is granted a right, and not involved in the political process granting that right, actions must be taken to enhance the outcome of the exercise of the right.

Sixteenth amendment:

The right of Congress to lay and collect taxes on incomes, from whatever source derived, without apportionment among the several states, and without regard to any census or enumeration. Note: among the several states, but does not address the income of individual citizens. Should the income tax be the "right of the member states", and then apportioned to the federal government?? Could have been written…."The Congress shall have the power to lay and collect taxes on any income source from individuals, businesses, business groups, charities and religious groups. Why would any earned income derived from the conduct of business be excused?

Seventeenth amendment:

Defines specifically the number of senators (2), how elected, length of term, and filling of vacancies. Note: possibly unconstitutional in view of Article V, Clause 3 of the constitution.

Eighteenth amendment:

Prohibition of the sale of intoxicating liquors

Nineteenth amendment:

The right to vote shall not be denied or abridged on account of sex

Twentieth amendment proposed:

Could be construed as an attempt to limit and control child labor. This article was never ratified.

Twentieth amendment:

Stipulated when the terms of the President, Vice-President and Congress would begin. Called for Congress to meet "at least once a year". It, also, specified the succession of the President and Vice-President. Note: the terminology of Vice-President elect

Twenty-first amendment:

Repealed the 18th prohibition amendment

Twenty-second: limited the number of times a person could be elected to the office of President to twice. Note: this simply violates the right to vote by denying choice. This is unconstitutional.

Twenty-third amendment:

Gave the rights granted the member states to the District of Columbia

Twenty-fourth amendment:

Abolished the poll tax, or any tax to vote, for any election to the federal government. Note: the language does not make a poll tax unconstitutional except in federal elections

Twenty-fifth amendment:

Specified the Vice-President would succeed to the Presidency if the President died or resigned. The appointment of a new Vice-President needs confirmation by a majority of both houses of congress. Note: here the Vice-President is not a selection by the President but by confirmation of the Congress

Twenty-sixth amendment:

Changed the voting age to 18 years of age. Note: what are the legal implications of granting citizenship voting rights?

Twenty-seventh amendment proposed:

The equal rights article. Proposed in 1972, expired unratified in 1982

Twenty-seventh amendment proposed:

Stipulating the District of Columbia shall be treated as though it were a State. Proposed in 1978, expired unratified in 1985.

Twenty-seventh amendment:

Compensation changes for senators and representatives will take effect only after the next election.

Conclusion

This manuscript has attempted to provide the reader with both a philosophical (Declaration of Independence) and legal (Constitution of the United States) foundation for the principles of the government of the United States of America. It is hoped this quick review will remind all who read it of the importance both historically and socially what was established by the founding fathers.

Thomas Paine wrote in *common sense in 1777,* "these are times that try men's souls…..what we obtain to lightly; it is dearness only that gives everything its value."

It is clear the Declaration and the Constitution desired the participation of the legal citizens of the United States. This is a Representative Democracy with citizens having "the right" to vote for representatives to represent them in their governance. Thomas Paine would remind us we have a "responsibility" to vote. All Americans should be endeared to our system of government. A tremendous price has been paid by revolution, civil strife and world wars.

This form of governement shall not be allowed to perish from this earth

Appendix 1

A look at national voter turnout in federal elections from 1960-2006 (info www.inforplease. com)

Year	Voting age population	Voter registration	Turnout of voting age pop. %	Voter turnout
1960	109.1M	64.8M	63.1	68.8M
1962	112.4M	65.4M	47.3	53.1M
1968	120.3M	81.7M	60.8	73.2M
1970	124.5M	82.5M	46.6	58.0M
1976	152.3M	105.0M	53.6	81.5M
1988	182.8M	126.4M	50.1	91.6M
2002	215.5M	151.0M	37.0	79.8M
2004	221.3M	174.8M	55.3	122.3M
2006	220.6M	135.9M	43.6	80.6M

Note: some voter registration not include

Note: high voter turnout represents presidential elections

Appendix 2

If America sets the standard for freedom to vote, and voting rights, the percentage of voter turnout in countries with no compulsory voting and ten elections on record from 1960 to 1995 would average approximately 76%. This is 20 percentage points increase over the United States voter turnout of eligible voters.

As a reference:

When Abraham Lincoln was elected president in 1860, the eligible voter turnout was 81.2%

Epilogue

Remember: let no law or political process be enacted that restricts the

Right
To
Vote

www.ingramcontent.com/pod-product-compliance
Lightning Source LLC
Chambersburg PA
CBHW031328290526
45784CB00014B/2429